CONSERVATION OF
CALIFORNIA WALNUT
IN THE EASTERN SANTA MONICA MOUNTAINS

Travis Longcore
Nina Noujdina

March 2022

Preferred citation:
Longcore, T., and N. Noujdina 2022. Conservation of California Walnut in the Eastern Santa Monica Mountains. The Urban Wildlands Group, Los Angeles, California.

For copies of this report, contact:
The Urban Wildlands Group
P.O. Box 24020
Los Angeles, California 90024-0020

A digital copy of this report is available at: http://www.urbanwildlands.org

TABLE OF CONTENTS

ACKNOWLEDGMENTS

We thank Diana Zogran for generously funding the preparation of this report, Catherine Rich for editing several versions of the manuscript and providing many useful suggestions, Dr. Alison Lipman, Brenton Spies, and their students at UCLA for their work expanding knowledge of the distribution of California walnut in the eastern Santa Monica Mountains, and Jason Casanova for designing the layout.

Cover photo: Claude Laprise

EXECUTIVE SUMMARY

California walnut *(Juglans californica)* is a rare species and keystone component of two Sensitive Natural Communities designated by the State of California: Coast Live Oak–California Walnut Woodland and California Walnut Groves. The species is under assault from residential and commercial development throughout its remaining range in southern California. In this report we address a region within the eastern Santa Monica Mountains that is subject to ongoing development pressure in which steep parcels are now being targeted for residential construction, threatening the remaining walnut groves and oak–walnut woodlands. The City of Los Angeles issues permits to remove California walnut trees at a rate of one mature tree every 7.2 days.

We present background information about the ecology, distribution, and conservation status of California walnut and review the mechanisms that should be, but are not, protecting it in the environmental review process under California law. Although the City of Los Angeles has a native tree protection ordinance, in practice the ordinance does not preclude removal of trees for development, does not provide for any replacement of habitat area, which would be essential

for mitigation of biological impacts, and does not even require that any replacement trees are of the same species as the species removed. As a result, the area supporting California walnut and its associated natural communities continues to shrink and become more fragmented.

To assist in conservation planning for California walnut, we developed screening maps for the species and its two related Sensitive Natural Communities. The maps are derived from high-resolution color aerial photographs of the study area. We used the location of known examples of many different tree species to create descriptions of the color characteristics of those species. We then used a series of spatial analysis techniques to create maps showing the locations of trees that share similar spectral profiles with confirmed California walnuts and coast live oaks and that therefore have an elevated likelihood of being one of the two species. We cross-checked these maps with existing efforts that mapped larger blocks of forest and woodland habitats. The maps should serve the role of screening during development and informing conservation planning for these rare habitats. If the maps show the likely presence of one or the other species, on-the-ground surveys should be under-taken to ascertain if the site does indeed support individual California walnut trees and either Coast Live Oak–California Walnut Woodland or California Walnut Groves and therefore require heightened scrutiny during development or priority for conservation.

Based on our review and analysis, we recommend steps to improve the chances of California walnut avoiding further declines and associated degrada-tion in its conservation status:

- **Encourage community documentation of presence of California walnut trees** to spread awareness about their protected status and inform environmental impact analysis;

- **Fix the City of Los Angeles CEQA review process** that currently exempts as "urban infill" projects that would have a significant adverse impact on the environment through loss of a rare species and Sensitive Natural Community;

- **Improve information available to consul-tants and landowners** to inform biological constraints analyses for properties within the range of California walnut;

- **Prioritize purchase of Coast Live Oak–California Walnut Woodland and California Walnut Groves** even if they are not part of the identified wildlife corridors that have motivated recent conservation purchases by State agencies; and

- **Expand analysis and conservation strategies to encompass the full geographic range of California walnut**, building from the tech-niques and analysis in this report.

Action is urgently needed because existing regulatory mechanisms, at least in the City of Los Angeles, are failing to protect this species.

INTRODUCTION

California walnut (*Juglans californica*) is recognized by the State of California as a rare species and is at risk of becoming endangered if the trends of habitat loss for the species continues. Yet, over the past three years, the City of Los Angeles has permitted the removal of this species at the rate of one mature tree every 7.2 days.[1] Although the City has a native tree protection ordinance, these trees are routinely permitted for removal to make way for new construction and expansion of existing homes. No habitat-based mitigation is required for these removals, and "replacement" trees for California walnut under the City ordinance are often of a different species unless conservation advocates intervene.

The City of Los Angeles has actively opposed protection of California walnut in court. When residents challenged the removal of California walnut associated with construction of a new home, the Los Angeles City Attorney asserted in briefs that California walnut did not qualify as a rare species.[2] To the contrary, the California Department of Fish and Wildlife (CDFW) recognizes California walnut as a rare species and the vegetation communities where it is present (Coast Live Oak–California Walnut Woodland and California Walnut Groves) as Sensitive Natural Communities that specifically must be considered during the environmental review process.

A substantial portion of the range of California walnut lies within the City of Los Angeles, where it faces a crisis. Planning and environmental review processes as implemented by current leadership have failed to afford the species the consideration required under State law, and rapid development and redevelopment of residential properties eats inexorably away at remaining

---

1. According to a review of reports from the Urban Forestry Division, removals were recommended to be approved by the Board of Public Works for 50, 95, and 30 California walnuts in the years 2018–2020, and 60 through mid-October 2021, representing one every 7.3, 3.8, 12.2, and 5.3 days (mean = 7.2 days).

2. Respondent's and Real Parties' Opposition Brief, *Friends of Westwanda Drive v. City of Los Angeles et al.*, Case No. 19STCP04113.

walnut habitats. An effective conservation approach is needed; these trends are accelerating in the current political climate that prioritizes housing development over sustainability.

The time to take conservation action to protect biodiversity is before a species becomes endangered. California walnut is a rare species that risks becoming endangered if current trends continue. The effective conservation of the natural communities associated with California walnuts depends on identifying their distribution so they can be appropriately mapped for environmental review and to identify candidate areas for land conservation. Current vegetation maps of the eastern Santa Monica Mountains identify larger habitat blocks, but the significant habitats remaining on developed and undeveloped parcels of smaller size are not mapped.

To provide additional guidance, we developed a high-resolution map of California walnut and coast live oak distribution in the eastern Santa Monica Mountains as a screening tool for environmental review and conservation. The purpose of the map is to identify trees within the study area that have a substantial probability of being either coast live oak or California walnut trees and consequently are either rare (California walnut) or make up natural communities that are considered sensitive. Given the large area compared with the resolution of the mapping effort (individual trees), a ground-verified survey was not possible. The maps, however, could be used early in the environmental review process to trigger site-level surveys to establish the identity of trees flagged on the maps.

In the sections that follow, we first provide background on California walnut and its ecology and conservation as an emblematically rare species in the City of Los Angeles. A substantial portion of its historical range lies within the City of Los Angeles, which increases the need for the City to protect it from existing threats. We then present the screening maps for California walnut and coast live oak vegetation communities, summarize the outputs compared with other descriptions of the distribution of coast live oak and California walnut, and discuss the potential use of the maps in conservation planning and environmental review. In the Appendix, we describe the approach for developing the screening maps, including the data and methods used and estimates of their accuracy compared with previous vegetation maps.

Ecology & Distribution of California Walnut

FIGURE 1. Characteristic deciduous leaves of California walnut in the eastern Santa Monica Mountains.

California walnut, also known as Southern California black walnut and California black walnut, is endemic to California, found naturally no other place on the planet. Plants are 10 to 70 feet tall (Jepson 1910, Munz 1973, Keeley 1990), in either tree form or as a shrub form of "really imposing size" (Jepson 1910).

California's walnut trees are unique in that they never form a single-species forest and only rarely a grove, but rather are often found in concert with oak trees (*Quercus* spp.). Unlike the shrubs of the coastal sage scrub, California walnut is a winter deciduous plant, losing its leaves in the winter (*Figure 1*).

Lifespan ranges to 100 years (Swanson 1967, Munz 1973, Keeley 1990). Trunk size and height are closely and significantly correlated with age (Quinn 1989, Keeley 1990). As the tree gets older, the blackish-brown bark becomes deeply furrowed (Munz 1973). Seed set begins at 5–8 years (Brinkman 1974). Seeds do not become dormant, but typically germinate within 4 weeks of dispersal (Brinkman 1974). Many seeds never grow because they are consumed by animals or carried by gravity, animals, or flood waters to unfavorable locations (Swanson 1967, Anderson 2002).

Habitat for the species is often described as north-facing slopes with deep soils and high clay content (Quinn 1989). In the Santa Monica Mountains, California walnut occurs with annual grasslands, native herbaceous vegetation, coastal sage scrub, north slope chaparral, or oaks (Quinn 1989, Tiszler and Rundel 2007). Studies regarding the Santa Monica Mountains and Los Angeles County report successful growth to occur on slopes with deep soil at elevations below 1,066 m (Horton 1949, Anderson 2002) (*Figure 2*). Walnut woodlands are suggested to occur in locations with springs or subsurface water available (Tiszler and Rundel 2007). As a winter deciduous plant that holds its leaves through the hot summer and fall months, access to water is important and the root system is extensive, often with a deep taproot (Miller 1976). This water need leads to an association between California walnut and riparian zones, intermittent streams, and moist canyons (Swanson 1967, Keeley 1990, Anderson 2002) (*Figure 3*), with reduced presence in drier locations or locations prone to drought and frequent fire (Anderson 2002). Nevertheless, walnuts can persist in drier areas with subsoil seepage and good water retention (Anderson 2002), such as through high clay content.

Planting of California walnut as a food source outside of its native range complicates the description of its native range. Once plants that were deliberately introduced are excluded, the native range of the species is focused in Ventura, Los Angeles, Orange, Riverside, and San Bernardino counties. Outlying stands are found in San Diego and Santa Barbara counties (Griffin and Critchfield 1972) (*Figure 4*). Within Los Angeles County, the largest contiguous range stretches across the Santa Monica Mountains and then north through northeast Los Angeles to the San Rafael Hills and Verdugo Hills (*Figure 5*). East of downtown Los Angeles, the range historically would have extended southeastward across the hills toward the Puente Hills and San Jose Hills, where another portion of the range is found (Ethington et al. 2020). Swanson (1967) reports the range extending across the San Fernando Valley northward from the northern slope of the Santa Monica Mountains (*Figure 6*). Similarly, California walnut is found in the foothills of the San Gabriel Mountains. It is difficult to

FIGURE 3. Example of fresh growth on a small grove of California walnuts along the bottom of a drainage on the southern slope of the eastern Santa Monica Mountains.

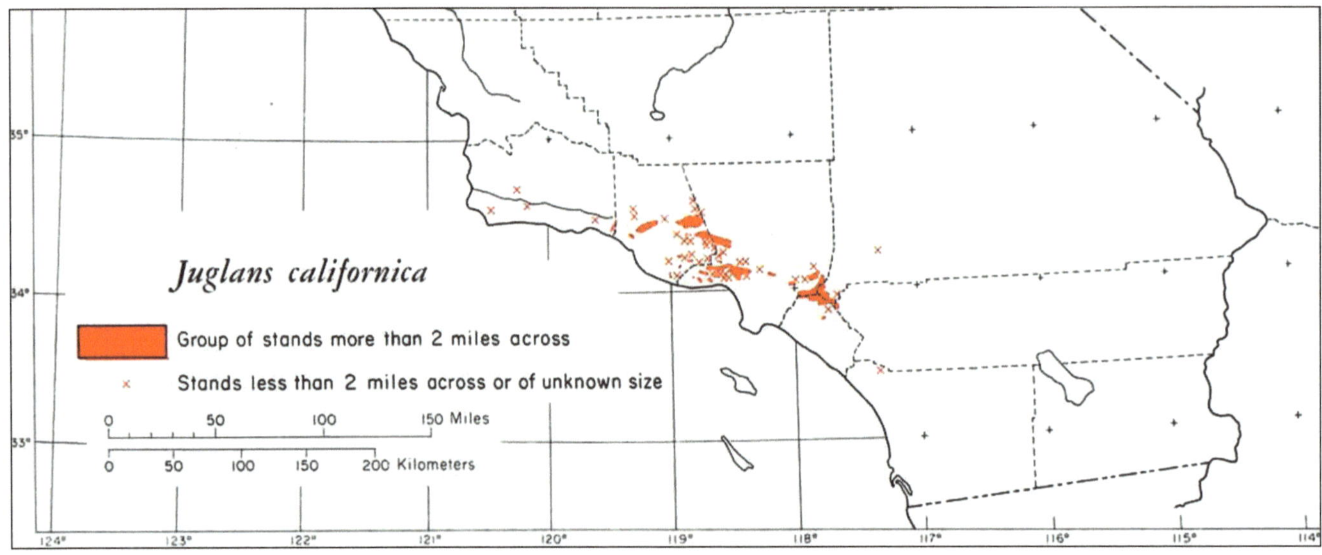

FIGURE 4. Rangewide distribution of *Juglans californica* (Griffin and Critchfield 1972).

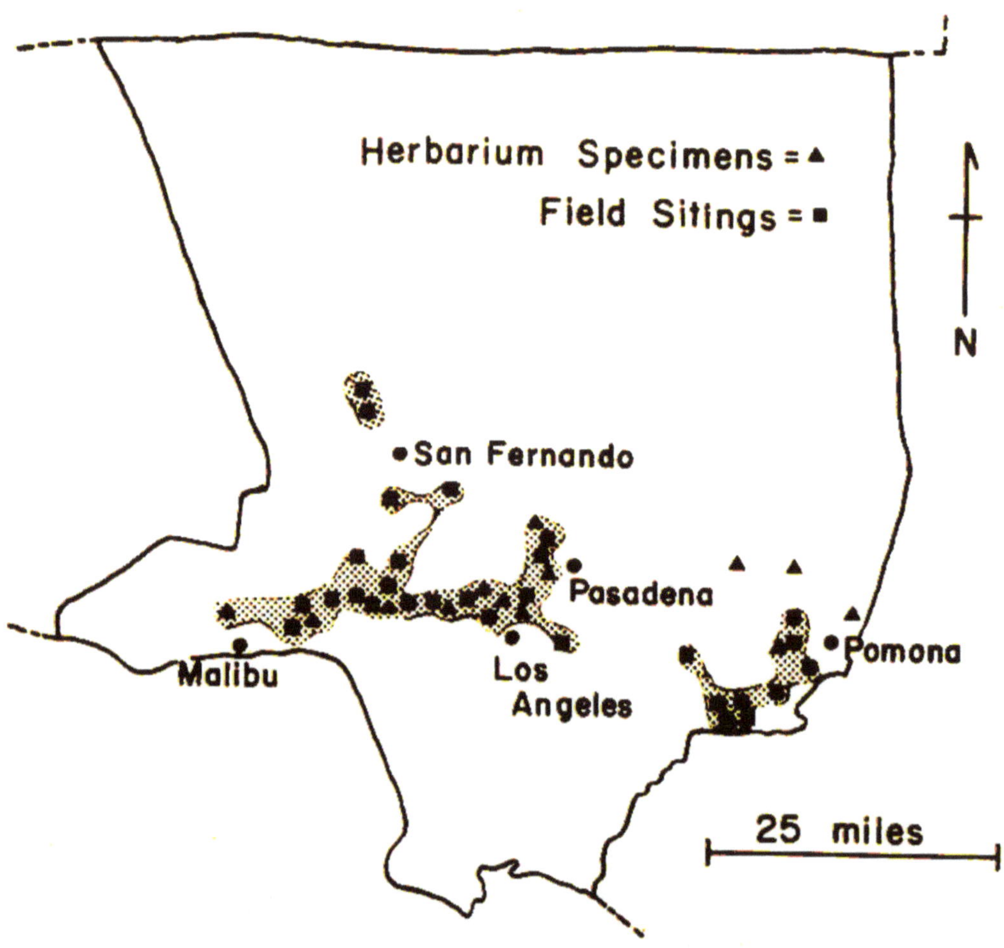

FIGURE 5. Distribution of *Juglans californica* in Los Angeles County (Swanson 1967).

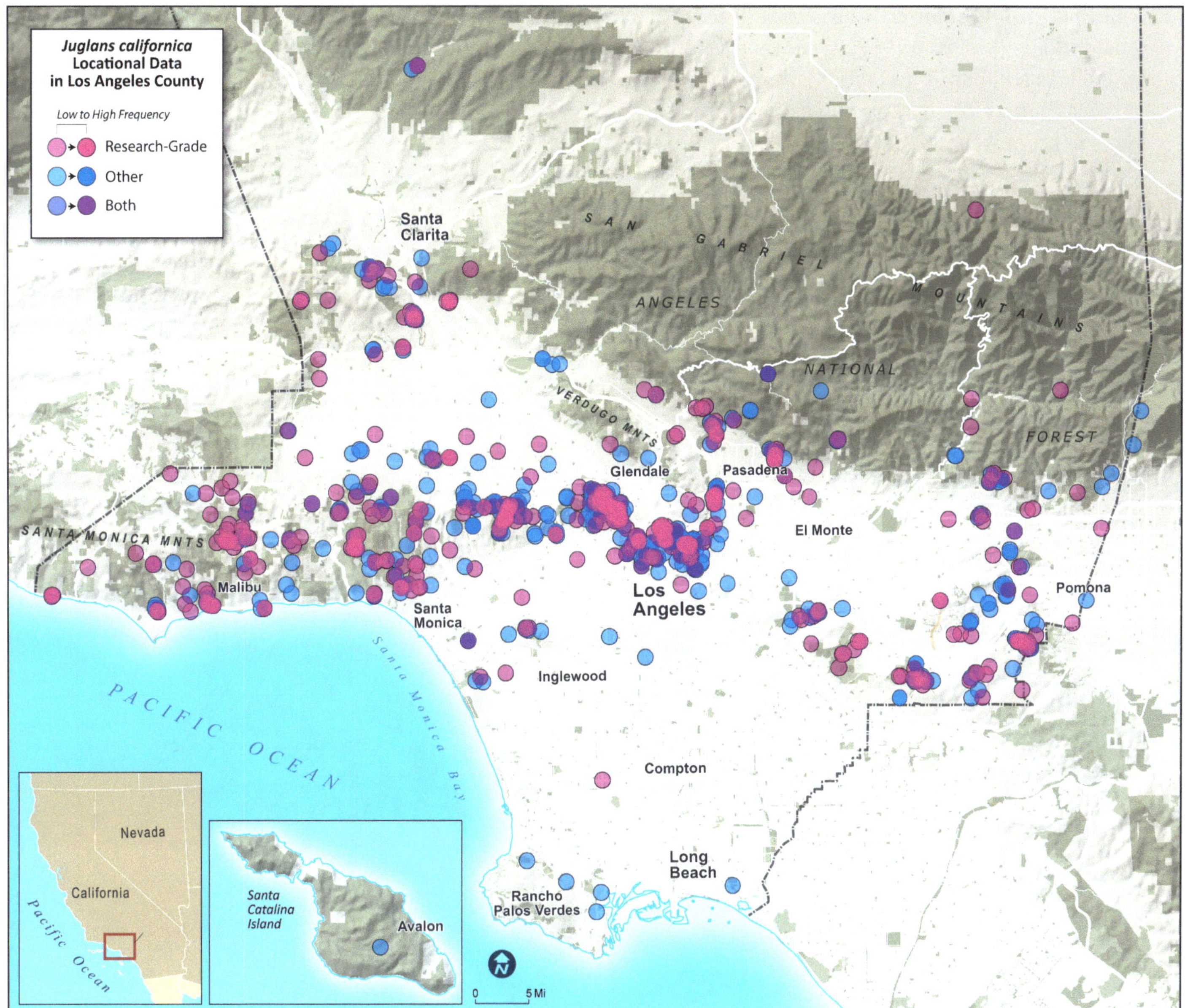

FIGURE 6. Summary of research-grade and other location data from herbarium and iNaturalist records for *Juglans californica* in Los Angeles County.

infer the full historical range of the species because so many localities were cleared for agriculture before any systematic surveys were undertaken. It is possible that the species found appropriate habitat and persisted along washes that extended from mountains into the alluvial fans and plains within these regions but those instances were lost without being documented. The Santa Monica Mountains include stands that are "among the largest remaining woodlands of *Juglans californica*" (Keeler-Wolf et al. 2007).

Walnuts are a food source for wildlife and the trees provide important three-dimensional complexity that transforms a grassland or shrubland into a forest. Their arching branches provide an interior environment that is excellent habitat for deer, nesting birds, and other wildlife (Quinn 1989). Western gray squirrels (*Sciurus griseus*) may still be present in the focal area of this study, and historically they would have consumed and dispersed walnuts. It appears unlikely that any of the fossorial rodent species (pocket gopher,

California ground squirrel) have jaws sufficient to open walnuts (Swanson 1967). California Scrub-Jay collects and buries just about any spherical object and therefore may play an important role in dispersal of walnuts (Grinnell 1936).

3 CONSERVATION STATUS OF CALIFORNIA WALNUT

The rarity and declining persistence of California walnut has been well documented for decades (Swanson 1967, Quinn 1989, Riordan et al. 2015). The IUCN ranks the species as "Near Threatened," which places it on the international Red List (Stritch and Barstow 2019). California walnuts occur mostly on private land and their small natural range has already been highly fragmented by urban development (Anderson 2002). As summarized 20 years ago:

> So far, the ability of California walnut to thrive on steep slopes has protected it, and much of its population survives in the Los Angeles conurbation on islands of habitat too steep and unstable on which to build. However, current "level-the-mountains" construction has wiped it out from even these habitats in many areas, especially the Puente Hills, and its future is uncertain (Anderson 2002).

Urbanization, and channelization of riverbeds and dry washes, has eliminated suitable habitat and fragmented persisting populations (Munz 1973). Using a climate-only habitat modeling approach, Riordan et al. (2015) mapped the presumed suitable conditions for *Juglans califor-*

nica and found that 31% of the mapped area was already urbanized. This result is almost certainly an underestimate of habitat loss because the climate-only model did not consider factors such as slope, aspect, and soils that restrict the species distribution, thereby overestimating the original habitat extent (Riordan et al. 2015).

Drought, exacerbated by climate change, habitat loss, and fragmentation all threaten the survival of California walnut (Munz 1973, Quinn 1989, Anderson 2002, Riordan et al. 2015). Adult trees resprout after fire and if cut down (Keeley 1990), which gives them some resilience in the face of fire and vegetation management to reduce fire risk. Increased fire frequency, however, threatens the species, because young trees are killed by fire (Anderson 2002).

To ascertain the potential threat of climate change on California walnut in the eastern Santa Monica Mountains, we compiled the downscaled and projected average maximum temperature and annual precipitation for a representative location in the middle of our focal area *(Figures 7-8)*. We plotted data from the RCP 8.5 scenario, which envisions that greenhouse gases will continue to increase through 2050 and plateau by 2100.

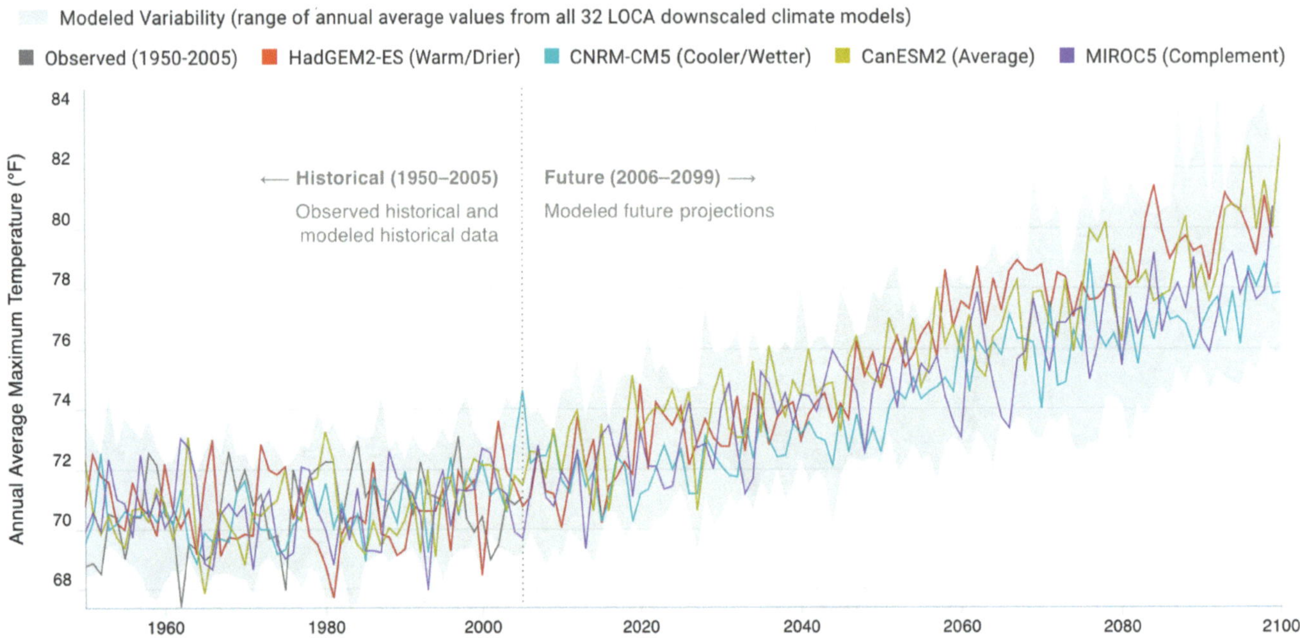

FIGURE 7. Average maximum temperature in the eastern Santa Monica Mountains. Observed record from 1950–2005. RCP 8.5 models simulated since 1950 and projected through 2100. Source: cal-adapt.org.

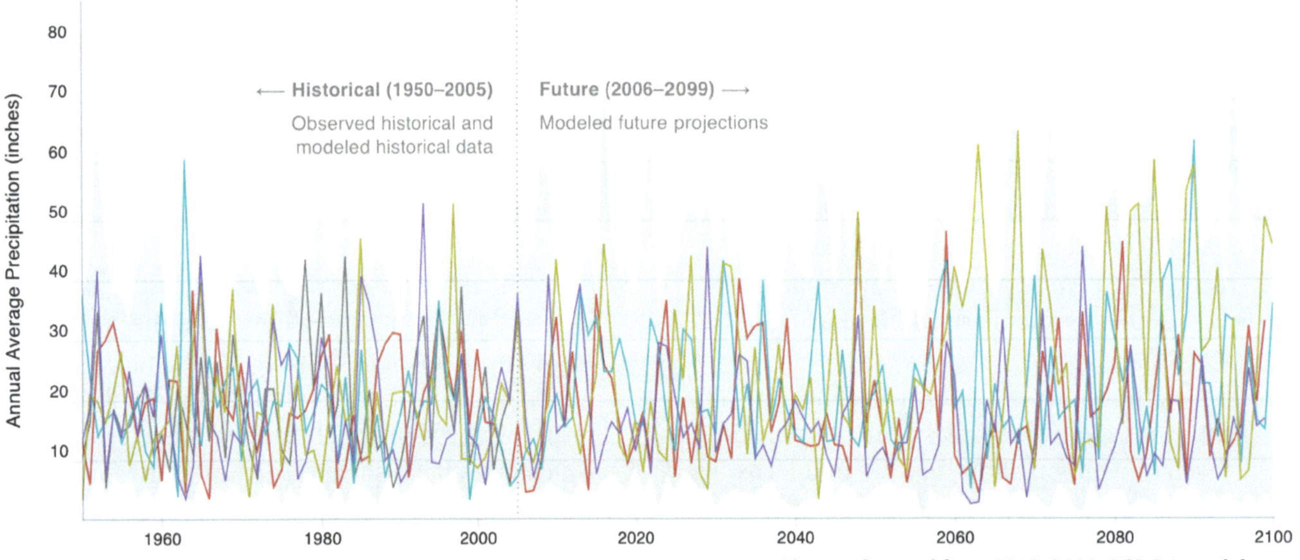

FIGURE 8. Average annual precipitation in the eastern Santa Monica Mountains. Observed record from 1950–2005. RCP 8.5 models simulated since 1950 and projected through 2100. Source: cal-adapt.org.

For average maximum temperature the predicted trend is uniformly upward, indicating a risk of greater drought stress, especially for seedlings that have not yet tapped into groundwater. For annual precipitation the models diverge considerably and on average predict a slight increase in precipitation. Together, assuming higher temperatures and equal or slightly higher precipitation, regeneration could be affected, and conservation of the cooler and moister north-facing slopes will be necessary. As climate changes, the period between regeneration opportunities will likely be longer as a result of higher temperatures resulting in higher moisture stress on seedlings. Preservation of existing mature trees will become more important so that they are producing walnuts that can establish when appropriate regeneration conditions are present. Multi-year droughts, when they occur, will present a threat, as has been previously identified (Keeley 1990).

CALIFORNIA WALNUT IN ENVIRONMENTAL REVIEW

California walnut has a California Rare Plant Rank of 4.2 (limited distribution and moderately threatened in California). This meets the definition of a rare species, and its status as a rare species has long been documented (Swanson 1967, Quinn 1989, Riordan et al. 2015). It is present on the official California "Special Vascular Plants, Bryophytes, and Lichens List"[1] for this reason. It is standard practice for species with a California Rare Plant Rank of 4 to be evaluated for impacts under CEQA as a sensitive natural resource, and this is routinely done in CEQA reviews issued by the City of Los Angeles for its own projects *(Table 1)*.

California walnut must be considered in CEQA review because it meets the criteria listed in Section 15380 of the CEQA Guidelines (14 CCR § 15380 (b)(2)), which defines a species as "rare" if:

(A) Although not presently threatened with extinction, the species is existing in such small numbers throughout all or a significant portion of its range that it may become endangered if its environment worsens; or (B) The species is likely to become endangered within the foreseeable future throughout all or a significant portion of its range and may be considered "threatened" as that term is used in the Federal Endangered Species Act.

---

1. https://nrm.dfg.ca.gov/FileHandler.ashx?DocumentID=109383

COMMON NAME *(Scientific Name)*	STATUS FEDERAL/STATE/CRPR	SPECIES DESCRIPTION
Southern California Black Walnut *(Juglans californica)*	-/-/4.2	The Southern California black walnut is a perennial deciduous tree that is found in chaparral, cismontane woodland, coastal scrub, and riparian woodland on slopes, and in canyons and alluvial habitats; 50–900 meters (164–2,952 feet). Blooming period: March – August.

TABLE 1. Example of consideration of California walnut as a rare species in CEQA analysis by the City of Los Angeles for its own program (Citywide Cat Program Draft Environmental Impact Report, 2019). This shows that the City of Los Angeles Bureau of Engineering, which prepared the report, recognizes the California Rare Plant Rank of 4.2 as requiring attention during review.

A species need not be formally listed as endangered or threatened to meet the criteria of Section 15380 of the CEQA Guidelines, even though the Los Angeles City Attorney recently argued exactly the opposite (incorrectly) in court.[2]

The City of Los Angeles, and other local jurisdictions, should look to the California Department of Fish and Wildlife for guidance on consideration of California walnut during review. CDFW has a special role as the Trustee Agency for biological resources during CEQA review (Fish and Game Code §§ 711.7 (a), 1802; Public Resources Code § 21070; California Environmental Quality Act [CEQA] Guidelines § 15386 (a)). CDFW unequivocally states that California walnut is a rare species under Section 15380 of the CEQA Guidelines:

> Southern California black walnut (*Juglans californica*) trees found on the Project site should be considered as a locally and regional rare, unique and/or uncommon (and/or) regionally rare plant species; that is, species that are rare or uncommon in a local or regional context, as such, would meet the CEQA definition of a rare species (CEQA § 15380). CEQA directs that a special emphasis be placed on "environmental resources" that are rare or unique to the region and would be affected by a proposed project [CEQA § 15125 (c)] or is so designated in local or regional plans, policies or ordinances (CEQA Guidelines, Appendix G). Public agencies have a duty under CEQA to avoid or minimize environmental damage and to give major consideration to preventing environmental damage (CEQA § 15021). Southern California black walnuts are California Native Plant Society (CNPS) Rank 4.2 and are considered locally sensitive species. In addition, the southern California black walnut is designated S3, which is considered vulnerable in the state

due to a restricted range with relative few populations. CDFW would consider loss of on-site populations of southern California black walnut to be potentially significant from a project and cumulative perspective under CEQA. Accordingly, impacts to these locally rare resources and adequate mitigation measures that reduce the impacts to less than significant should be described and incorporated … .[3]

The need to review impacts to California walnut habitat is further established through the status of the vegetation associations that have the species as a component part. All natural communities (defined as vegetation Alliances and Associations) that include *Juglans californica* are identified as Sensitive Natural Communities in the California Natural Community List from the California Department of Fish and Wildlife (*Table 2*).[4] CDFW requires consideration of impacts to Sensitive Natural Communities in environmental review:

> Natural Communities with ranks of S1-S3 are considered Sensitive Natural Communities to be addressed in the environmental review processes of CEQA and its equivalents.[5]

The City of Los Angeles has in recent years relied on compliance with its Protected Tree Ordinance to claim that impacts on California walnut and its Sensitive Natural Communities are mitigated. The ordinance, however, does not have mechanisms to mitigate such impacts. Measures that are tied to replacing individual protected trees, such as the City's Protected Tree Ordinance, do not provide adequate mitigation for Sensitive Natural Communities. Tree protection ordinances focus on individual trees, but CEQA analysis requires recognition of the whole

---

2. Respondent's and Real Parties' Opposition Brief, *Friends of Westwanda Drive v. City of Los Angeles, et al.*, Case No. 19STCP04113.

3. Letter from California Department of Fish and Wildlife commenting on Mt. San Antonio College 2015 Facilities Master Plan Update (FMPU) Supplemental Environmental Impact Report), dated August 8, 2016.

4. https://nrm.dfg.ca.gov/FileHandler.ashx?DocumentID=153398

5. https://wildlife.ca.gov/Data/VegCAMP/Natural-Communities#sensitive%20natural%20communities

CALIFORNIA CODE	ALLIANCE OR ASSOCIATION NAME	RARITY	SENSITIVE	HSV CLASS BREAK
61.130.18	*Populus fremontii – Juglans californica* Association			Y
72.100.00	California Walnut Groves Alliance	G3	S3	Y
72.100.03	*Juglans californica* / annual herbaceous Association	G3	S3	Y
72.100.04	*Juglans californica* / *Artemisia californica* / *Leymus condensatus* Association	G3	S3	Y
72.100.05	*Juglans californica* / *Ceanothus spinosus* Association	G3	S3	Y
72.100.06	*Juglans californica* / *Heteromeles arbutifolia* Association	G3	S3	Y
72.100.07	*Juglans californica* / *Malosma laurina* Association	GNR		Y
72.100.08	*Juglans californica* – *Quercus agrifolia* Association (includes former *Quercus agrifolia* – *Juglans californica* Association)	G3	S3	Y
74.100.11	*Umbellularia californica* – *Juglans californica* / *Ceanothus spinosus* Association	G3	S3	Y

TABLE 3. California Natural Communities (defined as vegetation Alliances and Associations) containing *Juglans californica* that are considered "sensitive" by California Department of Fish and Wildlife. G3: At moderate risk of extinction or elimination due to a restricted range, relatively few populations (often 80 or fewer), recent and widespread declines, or other factors. S3: Vulnerable in the state due to a restricted range, relatively few populations (often 80 or fewer), recent and widespread declines, or other factors making it vulnerable to extirpation. GNR: Global rank not yet assessed. Fremont Cottonwood – California Walnut Woodland (*Populus fremontii – Juglans californica* Association) is not currently assigned a rarity rank, but is identified as a Sensitive Natural Community, meaning that CDFW considers it to be at least S3 rarity.[6]

community of organisms that live within an area, in this instance within the oak–walnut woodland or walnut grove. Replacement of specimen trees on a site that has its habitat area significantly reduced to accommodate large structures does not offset the impacts to the recognized Sensitive Natural Community. The tree-based "replacement" program under the City of Los Angeles ordinance also does not require replacement of California walnuts with California walnuts, but rather routinely and nearly exclusively allows their replacement with coast live oak, resulting in a permanent and unmitigated loss of California walnut and its associated Sensitive Natural Communities *(Figure 9)*. Furthermore, the Protected Tree Ordinance pertains only to trees that have a 4-inch diameter at breast height and allows routine removal of California walnuts that are smaller than this size. As a result, California walnuts within fuel modification areas and on parcels that might be developed are never allowed to grow into mature trees and reproduce, impeding the ability of the species to sustain its numbers.

Replacing individual trees (even when they are the same species) but not habitat area is ineffective as a mitigation measure. Scientists have firmly established the predictable relationship between habitat area and the number of species supported by that area (Arrhenius 1921, Preston 1948). The relationship, referred to as the "species–area curve," is expressed by the equation $S = cA^z$ where S is number of species, A is area, and c and z are constants that vary by the ecosystem type and the geographic configuration of the area. If A decreases, then S also decreases. Some of the rich complement of oak–walnut woodland species will be eliminated from a site where the area of habitat is reduced, even if individual trees are planted as "replacements," because they do not make up for the loss of area. Furthermore, replacing individual trees does not replicate the preexisting structure and biodiversity of a vegetation Association. This has been known for years, and has previously been reviewed for oak woodlands:

---

6. *Id*. Elaborating on the methods for describing rarity, CDFW writes, "We have not ranked all associations with specific G and S ranks, except those defined from specific projects where they are well-understood geographically and so are more accurately ranked than placed within the broader "Sensitive" category. Natural Communities with ranks of 1–3 are considered sensitive and marked with a Y in the rightmost column."

Local jurisdictions also allow the removal of mature oaks in exchange for planting some greater number of smaller, sapling oaks. This contributes to the degradation of overall habitat values in three ways. First, the structural complexity of mature oaks will not be achieved by replacement specimens for decades. Second, mitigation plantings are often installed at sites that are not ecologically appropriate or in locations that will not be optimum for long-term viability. Monitoring of such mitigation plantings usually ceases after five years, far before replacement of the habitat values of the removed trees could ever even hope to be achieved. Third, mitigation plantings never include the associated understory species of an intact oak woodland (Longcore and Rich 2003).

Meaningful mitigation for impacts to a Sensitive Natural Community might involve on- or off-site permanent protection or restoration of the same habitat type at a specified mitigation ratio. A typical mitigation ratio for loss of a Sensitive Natural Community ranked S3 (all of those with *Juglans californica*) as usually recommended by CDFW would be 5:1 (in area/acreage). Avoidance of significant impacts on rare species and Sensitive Natural Communities is always the most desirable outcome. If impacts are unavoidable, an area-based mitigation scheme is required, with permanent protection, performance criteria, and enforceability, as part of CEQA compliance.

Screening Maps for California Walnut and Coast Live Oak

We developed screening maps for the eastern Santa Monica Mountain in an area bounded by the 405 Freeway on the west, Ventura Boulevard on the north, the 101 Freeway on the east through the Cahuenga Pass, and Sunset Boulevard on the south *(Figures 10-11)*. We produced maps with a 10-m grid showing the areas that are most likely to have either California walnut or coast live oak present within each grid cell. These represent the cells where our analysis of the vegetation height and spectral properties of each pixel within the cell returned the highest values for each species (see Appendix). These maps indicate, at the parcel scale, those locations that have the greatest probability of having each species present. They represent the highest confidence locations from the analysis.

For walnuts, the areas with the highest values are at greater elevation than the oaks. They include scattered 10-m cells within areas mapped on the north-facing slopes as walnut woodlands by the National Park Service, as would be expected. Substantial concentrations of probable walnut trees also are visible in Beverly Glen Canyon, Benedict Canyon, and Stone Canyon on the south-facing slope, along with pockets within residential neighborhoods on the north-facing slope in Studio City.

The distribution for 10-m grid cells with many probable oak tree pixels differs by extending farther south into the foothill neighborhoods just north of Sunset Boulevard and being more prevalent at these elevations. This pattern is consistent with descriptions of the historical ecology of the region that show a band of oak woodlands that extended historically east-west across the Santa Monica Mountains foothills, and which Indigenous peoples tended to maximize acorn production before European settlement (Ethington et al. 2020).

The differences between the areas of greater dominance of oaks and walnuts are visible in the 250-m resolution map *(Figure 12)*. At this resolution, the oak woodland band in the foothills is quite apparent, while walnuts have a greater extent at higher elevations. It should be noted, however, that even in those areas mapped as walnut woodlands, oaks are also found, and vice versa. This result should inform those doing field surveys for vegetation mapping to be prepared

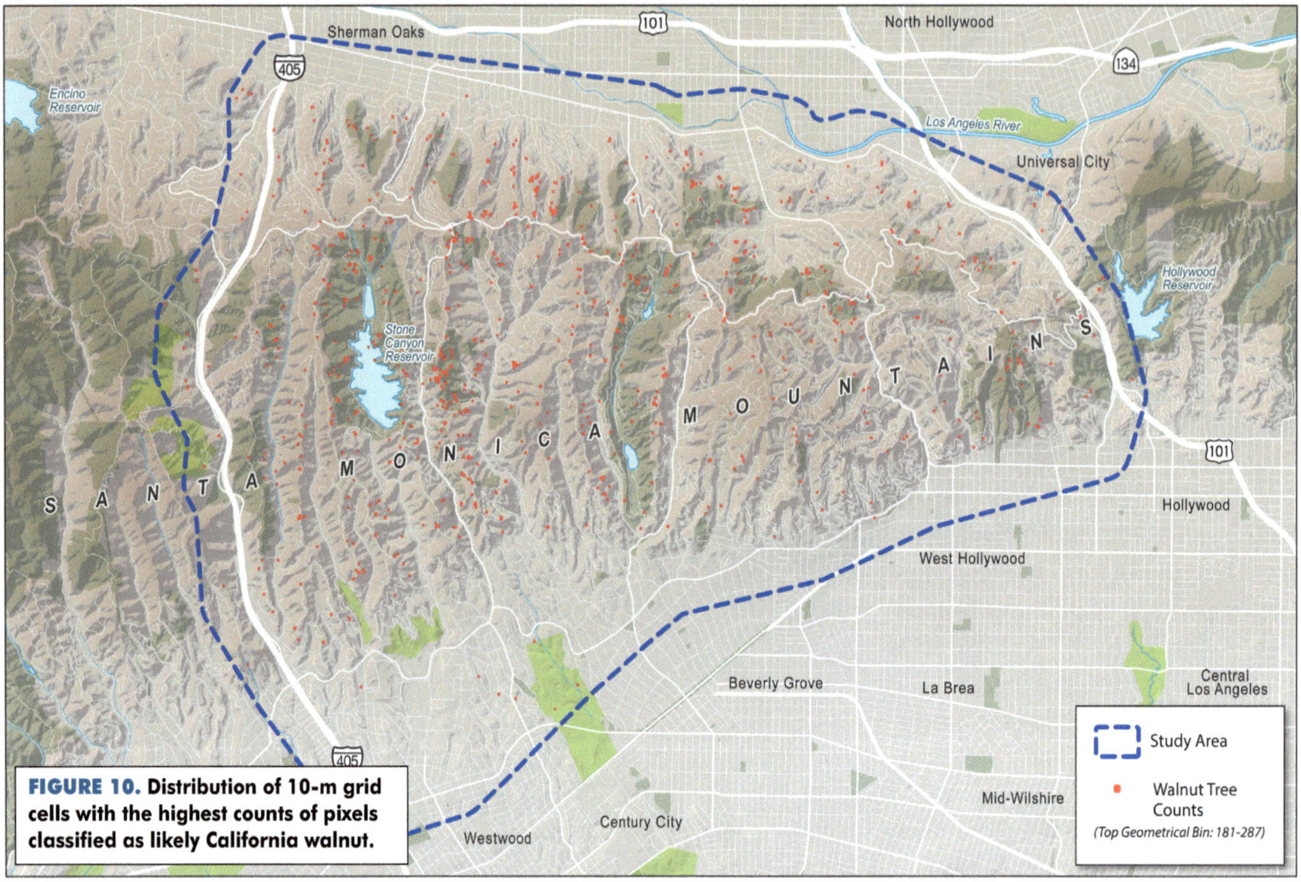

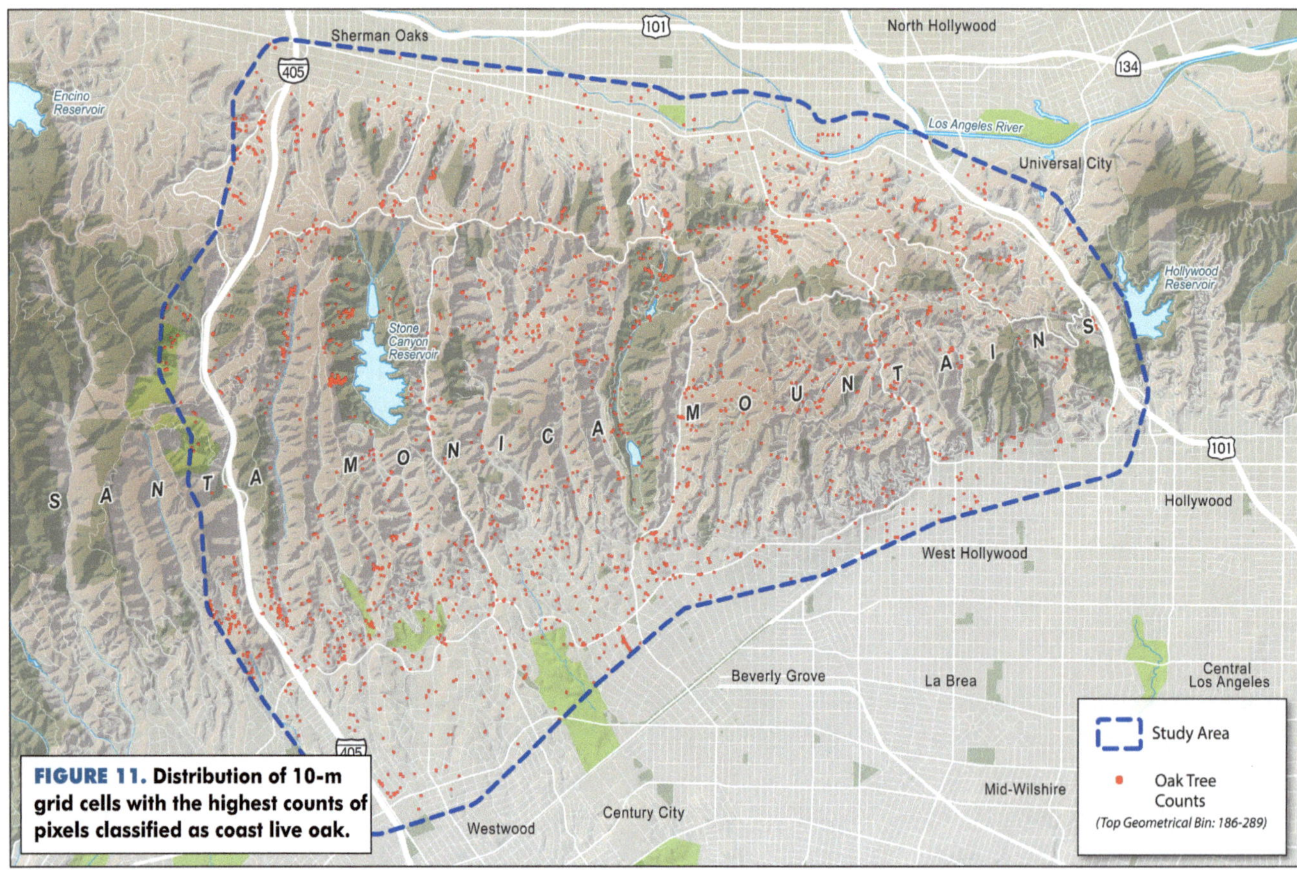

FIGURE 10. Distribution of 10-m grid cells with the highest counts of pixels classified as likely California walnut.

FIGURE 11. Distribution of 10-m grid cells with the highest counts of pixels classified as coast live oak.

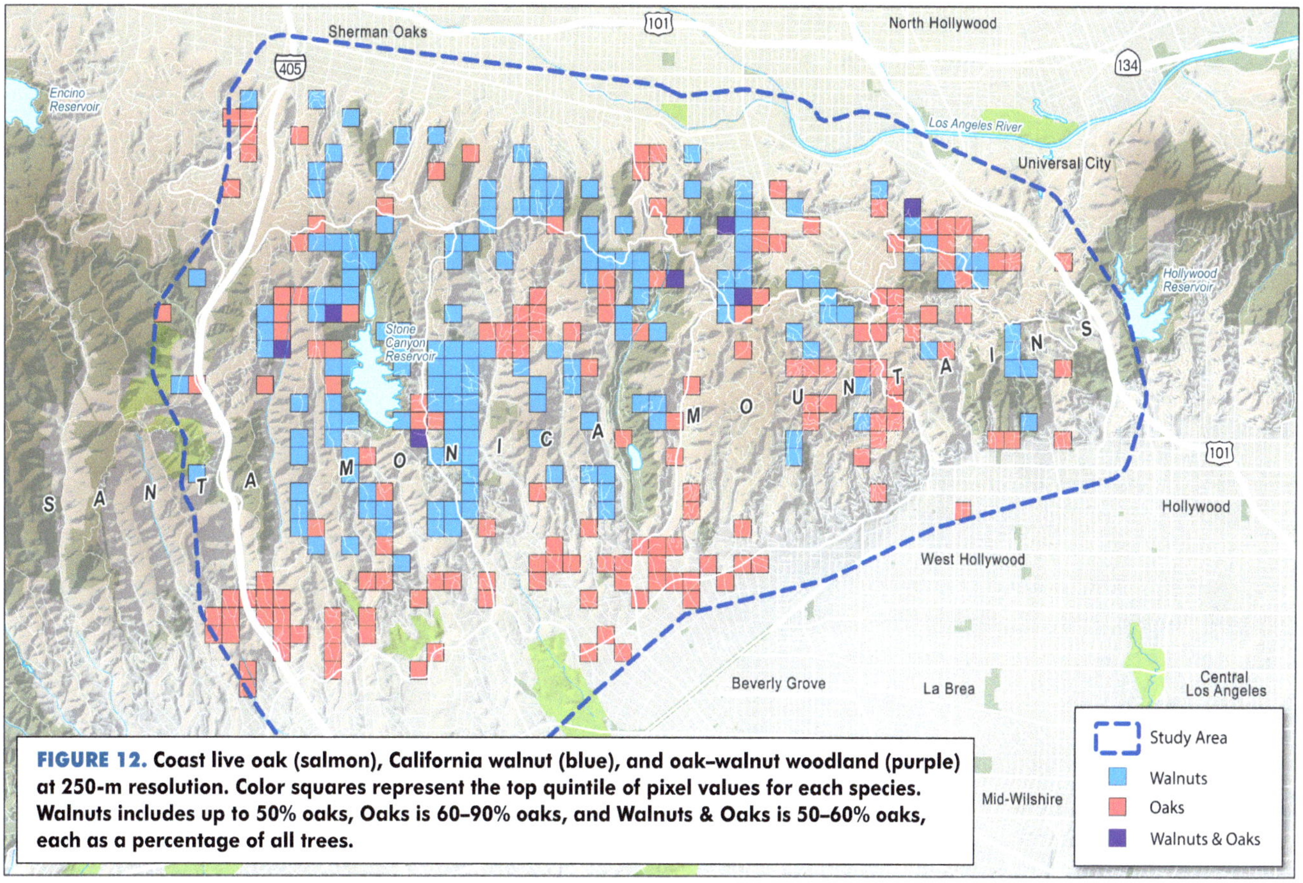

FIGURE 12. Coast live oak (salmon), California walnut (blue), and oak–walnut woodland (purple) at 250-m resolution. Color squares represent the top quintile of pixel values for each species. Walnuts includes up to 50% oaks, Oaks is 60–90% oaks, and Walnuts & Oaks is 50–60% oaks, each as a percentage of all trees.

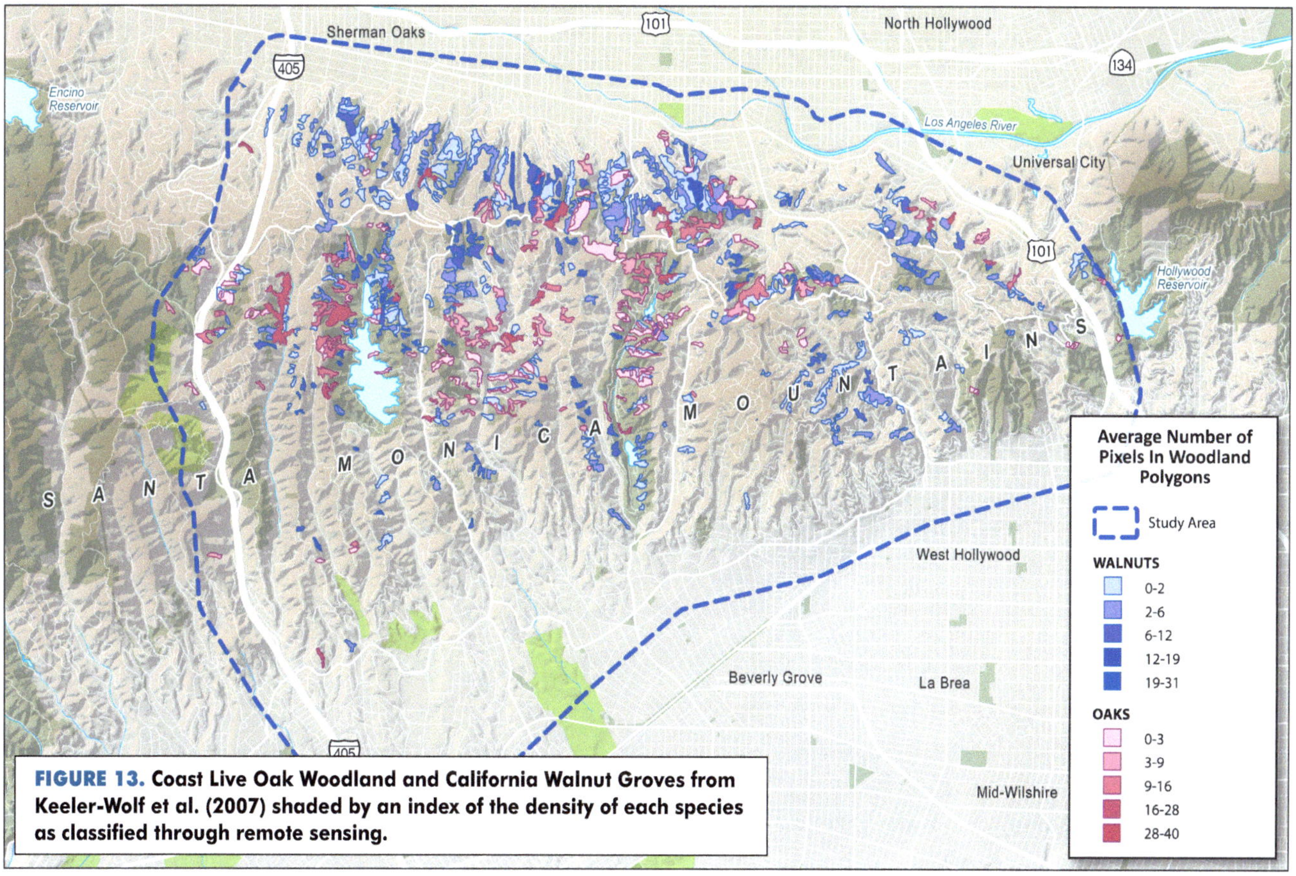

FIGURE 13. Coast Live Oak Woodland and California Walnut Groves from Keeler-Wolf et al. (2007) shaded by an index of the density of each species as classified through remote sensing.

to find mixed oak–walnut woodlands throughout the eastern Santa Monica Mountains and not only on north-facing slopes, which are typically associated most with walnut woodlands.

Our remote sensing approach focused on identifying locations that were likely to be individual walnut or oak trees and not on mapping and classifying vegetation communities. These are two different activities—vegetation mapping involves dividing the landscape up into relatively homogeneous and mutually exclusive units and then assigning each unit to a vegetation type based on the dominant species. Because rules for membership in a vegetation classification focus on the tallest vegetation, trees may define a mapped unit without having continuous cover. However, the two native species that we mapped certainly should be found within the vegetation communities California Walnut Groves and Coast Live Oak Woodland. We extracted these two communities from the vegetation map of the Santa Monica Mountains (Keeler-Wolf et al. 2007) and mapped the average number of pixels within 10-m grid cells in each polygon that we classified as either California walnut or coast live oak *(Figure 13)*. The resulting map shows the results graphically for walnuts within walnut woodlands and oaks within oak woodlands. We see that a few, but not many, of the walnut woodland polygons and a few of the oak woodland polygons have low counts for their respective species. Low pixel counts classified as walnut trees are more common for the walnut woodlands, which can be attributed to areas where walnuts are the dominant tree species but are spaced sparsely within the area.

As another assessment of our results compared with the NPS vegetation maps, we compared the average number of pixels of our presumed oak and walnut trees in each mapped walnut woodland and oak woodland polygon *(Figure 14)*. The average number of oak pixels in oak woodlands was significantly higher than walnut pixels. The median number of walnut pixels in walnut groves was higher with no significant difference from

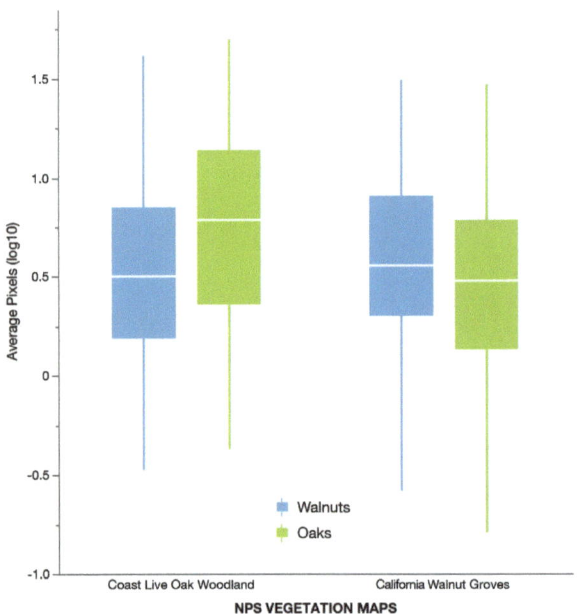

FIGURE 14. Average oak or walnut pixels (log scale) in polygons mapped as Coast Live Oak Woodland or California Walnut Groves.

oak pixels. This result is consistent with the membership criteria for walnut groves, in which walnuts only have to be 30% of relative cover if oaks are present (Sawyer et al. 2009). High presence of oak trees in vegetation mapped as walnut groves is to be expected.

RECOMMENDATIONS

Encourage Documentation of Walnut Trees by Community

The screening maps suggest a distribution of California walnut beyond the historical description of habitat on the north face of the Santa Monica Mountains. Confirmation of the screening maps and additional detail about the distribution of California walnut within the eastern Santa Monica Mountains would aid in planning and conservation efforts. Many of the locations used in this study were recorded in the iNaturalist app *(Figure 15)*. California walnut is conspicuous and easy to identify by residents and visitors. It may also be an indicator species for biological diversity within open spaces and neighborhoods. Conservation organizations, local jurisdictions, and CDFW should undertake an education campaign to inform the public, including municipal and county leaders, about the presence and importance of California walnut and encourage residents and visitors to photograph and upload geolocated observations of walnut trees across Ventura, Los Angeles, Orange, and Riverside counties to iNaturalist.

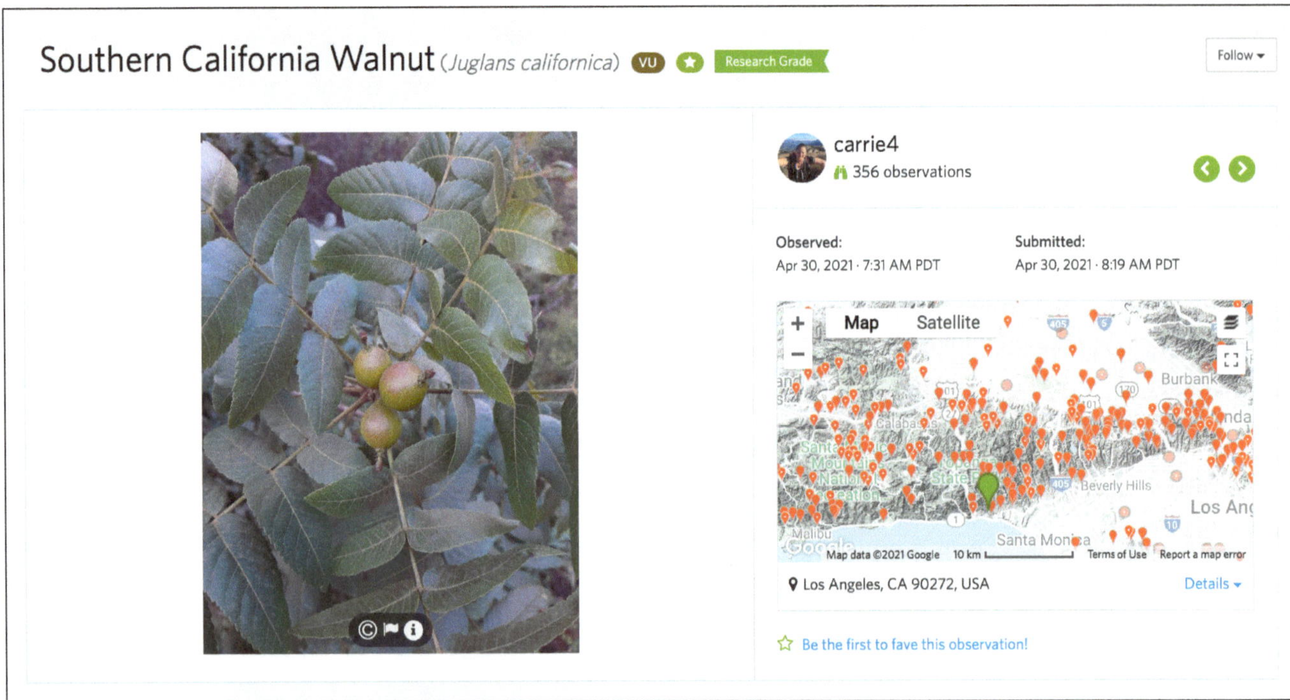

FIGURE 15. Example observation of *Juglans californica* on the iNaturalist website, indicating that it has a status of "vulnerable" (VU), is endemic to California (star), and that the observation has been confirmed by other naturalists (Research Grade).

Fix City of Los Angeles CEQA Review

Current City of Los Angeles CEQA practices exempt single-family home development from review, including in the eastern Santa Monica Mountains. A site that supports sufficient cover of California walnuts as part of a woodland should be recognized as being part of a State-recognized Sensitive Natural Community and mapped accordingly (see Sawyer et al. 2009). A Categorical Exemption from further review cannot be used for properties with a rare species or Sensitive Natural Community present because it can be concluded with certainty that loss of that habitat would constitute a significant adverse impact unless mitigated. The City of Los Angeles often points to its Protected Tree Ordinance in arguing that such development would not have impacts, but that regulatory tool only provides for replacement trees (which may not be of the same species), and not mitigation of the habitat area impacted at any ratio, let alone at the 5:1 mitigation ratio usually recommended by the California Department of Fish and Wildlife for Sensitive Natural Communities of this rarity.[1]

To stem the loss of this rare species and mitigate unavoidable losses, the City of Los Angeles should:

1. No longer use Categorical Exemptions for properties that contain vegetation that would be mapped as Sensitive Natural Communities (including all Alliances and Associations containing *Juglans californica*) under appropriate mapping protocols;

---

1. Kelly Schmoker-Stanphill, California Department of Fish and Wildlife, email to Travis Longcore dated November 27, 2019. Quoting from that email as an example of typical project-specific CDFW guidance on projects with Sensitive Natural Communities present: "The Department considers natural communities with ranks of S1–S3 to be sensitive natural communities that should be addressed in CEQA (CEQA Guidelines § 15125[c]). An S3 ranking indicates there are 21–80 occurrences of this community in existence in California, S2 has 6–20 occurrences and S1 has less than 6 occurrences. The Department recommends avoiding any sensitive natural communities found on the Project. If avoidance is not feasible, the Department recommends mitigating at a ratio of no less than 5:1 for impacts to S3 ranked communities and 7:1 for S2 communities. This ratio is for the acreage and the individual plants that comprise each unique community."

2. Avoid impacts to Sensitive Natural Communities and rare species where possible; and

3. Mitigate any impacts to Sensitive Natural Communities by protection or restoration of the same habitat type at a 5:1 mitigation ratio by acreage *and* tree number.

Improve Information About California Walnuts for Consultants and Landowners

The California Natural Diversity Database (CNDDB) and its online mapping tools are provided by CDFW to aid consultants and landowners in assessing the potential sensitive species that might be found on a particular property. For the eastern Santa Monica Mountains, the CNDDB includes only one single stand of *Juglans californica*, in Wilacre Park. More complete data in appropriate GIS formats are available for easy incorporation into the CNDDB and should be added, both from the map of the vegetation of the Santa Monica Mountains (Keeler-Wolf et al. 2007) and from the many research-grade observations on iNaturalist. The screening maps from this report and the National Park Service vegetation map will be shared with the public in an online tool (*bit.ly/SMMwalnuts*).

Prioritize Purchase of Sites Supporting California Walnut

Much of the current focus of local conservation efforts in the eastern Santa Monica Mountains is on the preservation of corridors for movement of large mammals (particularly mountain lion, bobcat, and mule deer). This goal is important but a focus solely on connectivity for larger mammals risks undermining conservation of rare species, including birds, that persist within the mosaic of developed and undeveloped parcels and have a greater conservation need in terms of species rarity. California walnut has a restricted range in southern California that is already dramatically reduced by urban development. It is threatened by both increasing temperatures and further residential construction within the very

topographically diverse landscapes that provide its greatest hope for suitable microclimates to persist in the face of climate change. Public and private conservation buyers should identify and target properties for acquisition or conservation easements that protect as much of the remaining distribution of California walnut as possible. This recommendation extends to parcels that are subject to fuel modification around structures because so long as the walnuts are not cut to the ground, they provide important habitat even with a cleared understory.

Expand Analysis and Conservation Strategies to Full Range of California Walnut

The mapping effort described here is limited to a portion of the range of California walnut as an example at the heart of the species range and to complement the current planning effort by the City of Los Angeles in its "Wildlife Pilot Study." The species would benefit from a range-wide assessment of the current distribution and threats from development. It is likely that similar development patterns and environmental changes threaten the species in areas other than the Wildlife Pilot Study area, both in and out of the City of Los Angeles. For example, the rapidly redeveloping areas of Mount Washington, Monterey Hills, and southwest toward Rose Hills and the Puente Hills are also important centers of California walnut distribution and are at risk because of the ineffectiveness of the current environmental review process. There are also remnant walnut groves in alluvial soils in the San Fernando Valley that are neither mapped nor given appropriate consideration in environmental review. Currently, the Los Angeles Zoo is proposing to expand into California walnut habitat.

Cooperation between local land trusts, regional land conservation agencies (such as the State conservancies), the California Department of Fish and Wildlife, and municipal planners and decisionmakers should chart a course now to protect the remaining distribution of California walnut and ensure that it does not become more imperiled than it already is. If coordinated action is delayed, stabilizing and recovering the species will become more difficult. Increased coordination and planning in support of this uniquely southern Californian species and its habitat is long overdue.

LITERATURE CITED

Anderson, E. N. 2002. Some preliminary observations on the California black walnut (*Juglans californica*). *Fremontia* 30:12–19.

Arrhenius, O. 1921. Species and area. *Journal of Ecology* 9:95–99.

Brinkman, K. A. 1974. *Juglans* L. Walnut. Pages 454–459 *in* C. S. Schopmeyer, editor. *Seeds of the Woody Plants of the United States. Agriculture Handbook No. 450*. Forest Service, U.S. Department of Agriculture, Washington, D.C.

Dagit, R., T. Hartwig, C. Simon, J. Decruyenaere, D. LeFer, T. Scott, M. Witter, M. Ferriter, L. Jessup, R. Ly, and J. Spector. 2019. Los Angeles County Native Tree Priority Planting Plan for the Santa Monica Mountains National Recreation Area. Final Report for Los Angeles County Contract #SPF03-03. Resource Conservation District of the Santa Monica Mountains, Topanga, California.

Dudek. 2019. Draft Beverly Hills Very High Fire Hazard Severity Zone Tree Related Fire Hazards. Dudek, Pasadena, California.

Espitia, Y., A. Hernandez, S. Hui, K. Khodadoostan, and N. Le. 2020. Mapping Southern California Black Walnut (*Juglans californica*) [unpublished practicum report]. UCLA Department of Ecology and Evolutionary Biology, Los Angeles.

Ethington, P. J., B. MacDonald, G. Stein, W. Deverell, and T. Longcore. 2020. Historical Ecology of the Los Angeles River Watershed and Environs: Infrastructure for a Comprehensive Analysis. University of Southern California Spatial Sciences Institute, Los Angeles.

Gauch, H. G. 1982. *Multivariate methods in community ecology*. Cambridge University Press, New York.

Griffin, J. R., and W. B. Critchfield. 1972. The Distribution of Forest Trees in California. USDA Forest Service Research Paper PSW-82. Pacific Southwest Forest and Range Experiment Station, Forest Service, U.S. Department of Agriculture, Berkeley, California.

Grinnell, J. 1936. Up-hill planters. *The Condor* 38:80–82.

Horton, J. S. 1949. Trees and Shrubs for Erosion Control in Southern California Mountains. State of California and California Forest and Range Experiment Station, U.S. Forest Service, Sacramento.

Houborg, R., J. B. Fisher, and A. K. Skidmore. 2015. Advances in remote sensing of vegetation function and traits. *International Journal of Applied Earth Observation and Geoinformation* 43:1–6.

Jepson, W. L. 1910. *The Silva of California*. The University Press, Berkeley.

Keeler-Wolf, T., J. Evens, J. Christian, R. Taylor, E. Reyes, and J. Tiszler. 2007. A vegetation classification for the Santa Monica Mountains. Pages 131–157 *in* D. A. Knapp, editor. *Flora and Ecology of the Santa Monica Mountains*. Southern California Botanists, Fullerton, California.

Keeley, J. E. 1990. Demographic structure of California black walnut (*Juglans californica*; Juglandaceae) woodlands in Southern California. *Madroño* 37:237–248.

Longcore, T., and C. Rich. 2003. Urban oaks and urban oak woodlands. *Oaks* [newsletter]. California Oak Foundation, Berkeley, California.

Miller, R. B. 1976. Wood anatomy and identification of species of *Juglans*. *Botanical Gazette* 137:368–377.

Munz, P. A. 1973. *A California flora and supplement*. University of California Press, Berkeley.

Preston, F. W. 1948. The commonness, and rarity, of species. *Ecology* 29:254–283.

Quinn, R. D. 1989. The status of walnut forests and woodlands (*Juglans californica*) in southern California. Pages 42–54 *in* A. A. Schoenherr, editor. *Endangered Plant Communities of Southern California*. Southern California Botanists, Claremont, California.

Riordan, E. C., T. W. Gillespie, L. Pitcher, S. S. Pincetl, G. D. Jenerette, and D. E. Pataki. 2015. Threats of future climate change and land use to vulnerable tree species native to Southern California. *Environmental Conservation* 42:127–138.

Sawyer, J. O., T. Keeler-Wolf, and J. Evens. 2009. *A Manual of California Vegetation*. Second edition. California Native Plant Society, Sacramento.

Stritch, L., and M. Barstow. 2019. *Juglans californica*, southern California black walnut. *The IUCN Red List of Threatened Species* 2019: e.T35154A61524825.

Swanson, C. J. 1967. The Ecology and Distribution of *Juglans californica* Wats. in Southern California. California State College at Los Angeles, Los Angeles.

Tiszler, J., and P. W. Rundel. 2007. Santa Monica Mountains: biogeography and cultural history. Pages 1–16 *in* D. A. Knapp, editor. *Flora and Ecology of the Santa Monica Mountains*. Southern California Botanists, Fullerton, California.

Tucker, C. J. 1979. Red and photographic infrared linear combinations for monitoring vegetation. *Remote Sensing of Environment* 8:127–150.

Appendix: Methods for Development of Screening Maps

We used geospatial layers obtained from two different sources, the National Agriculture Imagery Program (NAIP) and the Los Angeles Region Imagery Acquisition Consortium (LARIAC).

NAIP imagery is collected during low cloud cover (<10%) during a "leaf-on" season with a 0.6-meter spatial resolution, and has four spectral bands corresponding to the blue, green, red, and near-infrared regions of the spectrum. The near-infrared region is especially valuable when studying vegetation because it provides information about chlorophyll content in plants and thus can be used to assess vegetation health, as well as to identify vegetation life forms and species. The 2016 imagery was collected during June, and the 2018 imagery during July. Both datasets were collected during a "leaf-on" season, but 2016 was a drought year and 2018 was not. These two datasets together facilitate use of differences in drought response of the target species to distinguish among them.

LARIAC data contained 4-band 4-inch ortho-imagery, collected in 2017, and a 0.9-meter digital elevation model (DEM) with its derivatives (Slope, Aspect, Height Above Ground (HAG)).

Training and testing locations for coast live oak and California walnut trees were obtained from GPS points collected by students involved in a research project at UCLA (Espitia et al. 2020), research-grade community observations recorded on the iNaturalist.org platform, and visual inspection using Google Street View.

In addition, we used habitat suitability maps created for the Los Angeles County Native Tree Restoration Mitigation and Priority Planting Plan (Dagit et al. 2019), vegetation maps for the Santa Monica Mountains National Recreation Area (Keeler-Wolf et al. 2007), and maps from a preliminary assessment of fire hazard from street trees in Beverly Hills (Dudek 2019).

Processing and Classification

Screening maps were created in several steps (*Figure 16*). The steps were as follows: 1) aligning and resampling available imagery, 2) building a tree mask, 3) creating a training set, 4) creating a raster dataset (data transformation), 5) image classification, and 6) evaluation of results. The whole process was iterative, with each step tightly intertwined with the other steps.

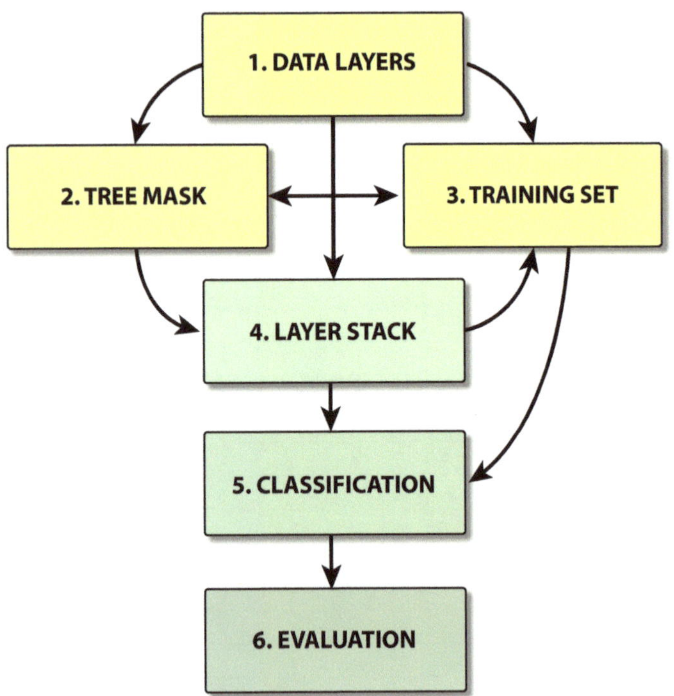

FIGURE 16. Schematic of workflow. Boxes 1, 2, and 3 describe three initial tasks that were carried out in parallel.

The data layers, such as 2-year NAIP imagery and HAG, were resampled to match NAIP pixel size. Each of the NAIP 4-band images was used to calculate a normalized difference vegetation index (NDVI) for its respective year. NDVI is a spectral ratio that is widely accepted by the remote sensing community to assess vegetation health via chlorophyll content (Tucker 1979, Houborg et al. 2015).

We then created a mask that excluded pixels of non-vegetated substrate and shorter vegetation types, such as grass and shrubs. In doing so, we applied a threshold to HAG and thresholds to both years of NDVI layers and reasoned that trees would have height greater than 6.5 feet AND have the NDVI value above 80% in at least one of the years. These parameters worked well to exclude short features (either natural or human-made) as well as tall features of a non-vegetative nature such as buildings and bridges. For example, a mask resulting from a threshold applied to NDVI only would include a grassy

sports field along with trees. The HAG layer alone, when thresholded with 6.5 feet, would include both trees and tall buildings, but when these two layers were added together, unwanted categories, such as grass and buildings, were eliminated (*Figure 17*).

Most data points for the locations of coast live oak and California walnut trees were downloaded from iNaturalist.org. Data from this website and its associated mobile device application are increasingly extensive as the platform grows in popularity with both community-based nature enthusiasts and professional scientists. The available data, however, must be carefully examined and filtered; GPS data collected for different purposes, with the use of different instruments, in some cases by enthusiasts with little expertise, may carry locational and identification errors. For example, a short tree that is growing under the crown of a larger tree would have no value for our project, in which we are interested in trees that are clearly seen from the sky. It may, however, may be very valuable for vegetation community studies. The iNaturalist dataset comes with rich metadata, including locations, photos, locational accuracy, quality (research grade or not), and other attributes. We thoroughly examined the dataset, leaving only points identified as research grade and with locational accuracy better than 20 meters. We further reduced the dataset to have only points that fall within our tree mask, were not overshadowed by other vegetation, and were confidently identified as target species. In addition to coast live oak and California walnut we built datasets for common species that occur in natural and urban parts of the study area: California sycamore (*Platanus racemosa*), arroyo willow (*Salix lasiolepis*), Mexican elderberry (*Sambucus mexicana*), blue gum tree (*Eucalyptus globulus*), Canary Island pine (*Pinus canariensis*), and cypress (*Cupressus sempervirens*).

We then built a training set that contained several tree species. That involved building a dendrogram and eliminating points that pre-

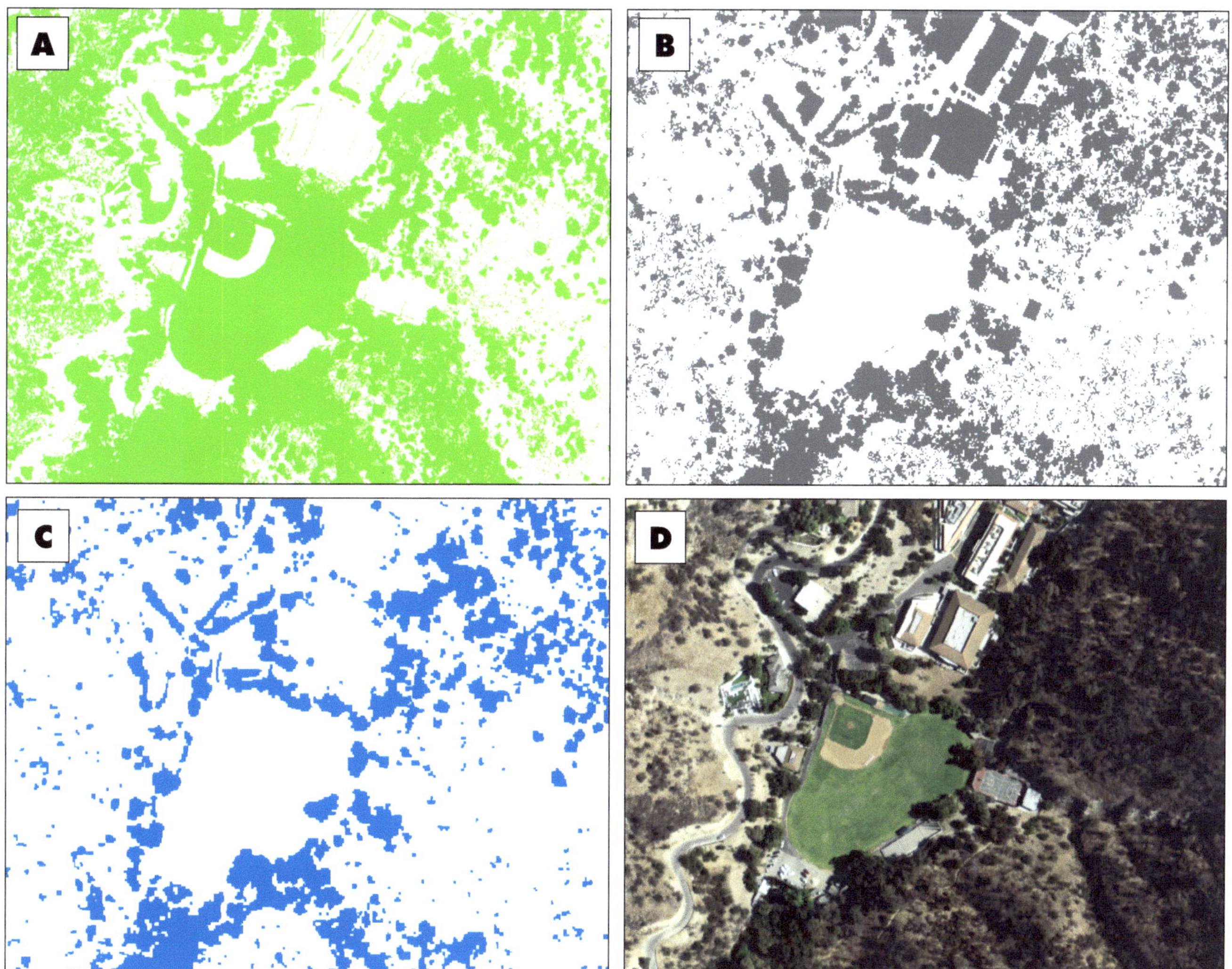

FIGURE 17. Tree map as a combination of spectral index and height above ground layers. (A) NDVI > 0.8; (B) HAG > 6.5 feet; (C) combination of (A) and (B); (D) NAIP image.

sented high confusion with other species' spectral signatures. Simultaneously with this process, we tested classification performance on different combinations of layers. We first created a layer stack of the most relevant layers, two years of NAIP imagery and a HAG raster, which were subjected to Principal Component Analysis (PCA). PCA is usually used to reduce heavy datasets with redundant variables (Gauch 1982). It transforms the original dataset into a new coordinate system with new uncorrelated variables, still preserving most of the information present in the original dataset. The first three components of PCA account for 95 percent of data variation. We applied an image segmentation tool to one of the PCA bands to create a thematic raster that would facilitate capturing shapes of different

objects. Building the training set was a process that involved frequently cross-examining multiple datasets: the tree mask, NDVI-2016, NDVI-2018, LARIAC, and PCA.

The final dataset that was used for classification consisted of a 4-band raster: three PCA bands (containing information about vegetation health and height above ground), and a thematic raster resulting from segmentation. The PCA transformation distinguishes trees of different species that appear similar in regular color imagery (*Figure 18*).

After the three main components of the analysis (raster dataset, training points, and tree mask) were completed, we performed image classifica-

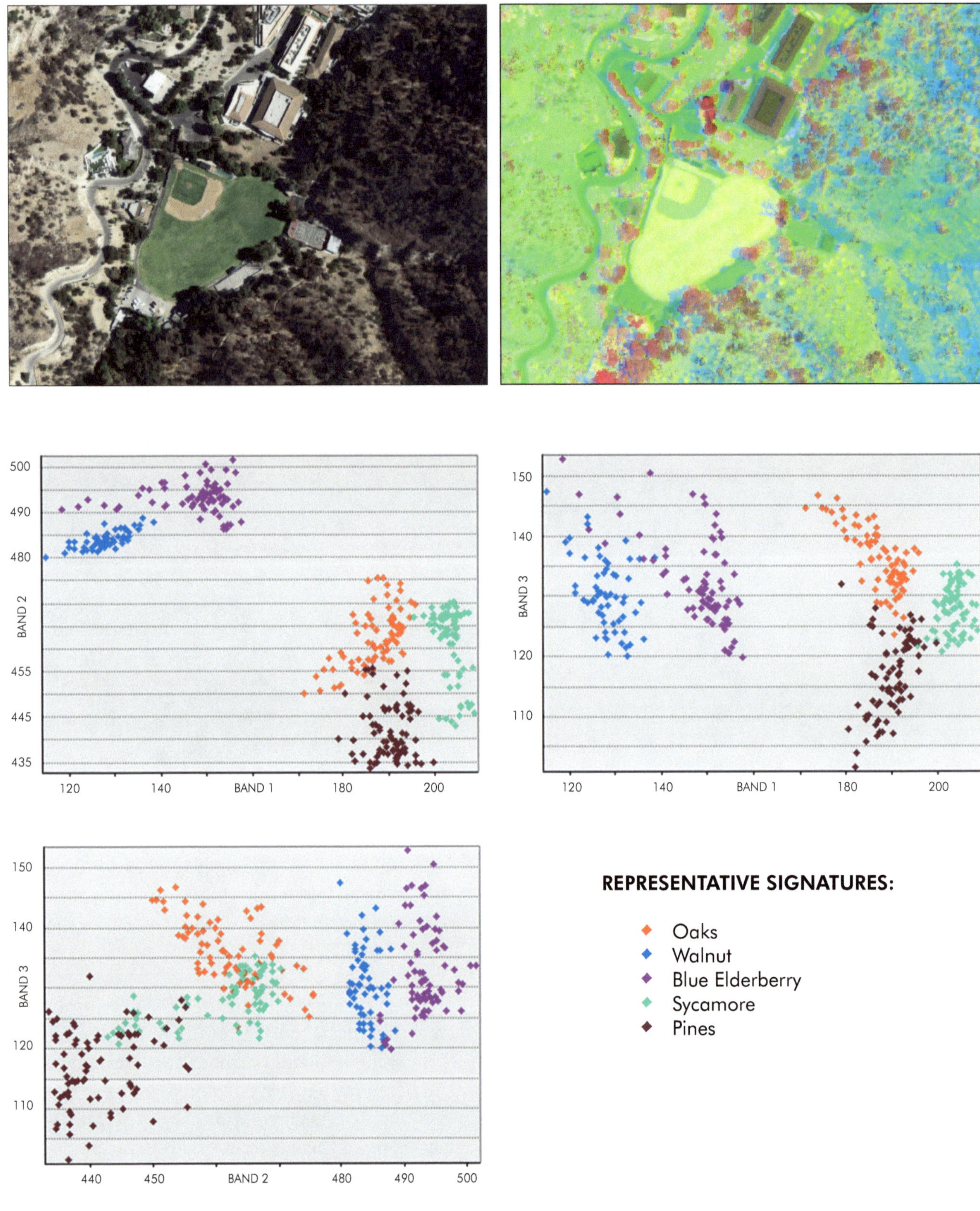

FIGURE 18. NAIP image *(top left)*; PCA raster *(top right)*; signatures of different tree species *(bottom)*.

tion using a Maximum Likelihood Classification (MLC) algorithm. MLC is the most widely used method in remote sensing. It assumes normal distribution of statistics in each class and assigns each pixel a specific class based on its highest probability. The study area contains a vast variety of trees, both naturally growing in parks and planted ornamentally in residential areas. It would be impractical to collect data for all tree species that occur within the study area, thus we added several that are most common, and in the end categorized them as "other." This step reduced confusion between oaks, walnuts, and other trees.

We then applied post-classification smoothing to eliminate a "salt-and-pepper" effect resulting from pixel-based classification. The method is used to erase speckle pixels, smooth class boundaries, and to clump nearby pixels belonging to the same class.

To visualize the results, we overlayed the classified pixels within different levels of the hierarchical Military Grid Reference System (MGRS) cells at different resolutions. The number of pixels for each species within cells at different resolutions were then visualized within ArcMap.

To validate the results, we compared our pixel-level classification with existing maps of oak and walnut woodlands at the vegetation Alliance level (Keeler-Wolf et al. 2007). Although this is a comparison between mapping of individual plant presences against mapping of a vegetation community, the comparison of the two vegetation communities should show greater oak presence in the oak woodlands and greater walnut presence in the walnut woodlands. We first summed the number of pixels probable for each species within the MGRS 10-m grids and omitted those grid cells with fewer than 76 probable pixels to focus on those cells mostly likely to have substantial cover of either species. We then took the average of the number of probable pixels within each vegetation Alliance polygon and compared them.

All data processing, including cleaning the original raw data, cross-referencing with high resolution imagery, data transformation, segmentation and classification, filtering and smoothing, were completed with ESRI ArcMap 10.7.

www.ingramcontent.com/pod-product-compliance
Lightning Source LLC
Chambersburg PA
CBHW042010110726
48006CB00004B/1038